S0-BBX-980

J.

DISNEY · PIXAR

RATATOUILLE
(rat·a·too·ee)

TOKYOPOP®

HAMBURG · LOS ANGELES · LONDON · TOKYO

Contributing Editor - Amy Court-Kaemon
Graphic Designer and Letterer - Tomás Montalvo-Lagos
Cover Designer - Lindsay Seligman

Digital Imaging Manager - Chris Buford
Production Manager - Elisabeth Brizzi
Senior Designer - Christian Lownds
Senior Editor - Julie Taylor
Managing Editor - Vy Nguyen
Editor-in-Chief - Rob Tokar
Creative Director - Anne Marie Horne
Publisher - Mike Kiley
President & C.O.O. - John Parker
C.E.O. & Chief Creative Officer - Stuart Levy

E-mail: info@TOKYOPOP.com
Come visit us online at www.TOKYOPOP.com

A ⊙TOKYOPOP® Cine-Manga® Book
TOKYOPOP Inc.
5900 Wilshire Blvd., Suite 2000
Los Angeles, CA 90036

Ratatouille

ISBN: 978-1-4278-0087-9

First TOKYOPOP® printing: October 2007

10 9 8 7 6 5 4 3 2 1

Printed in the USA

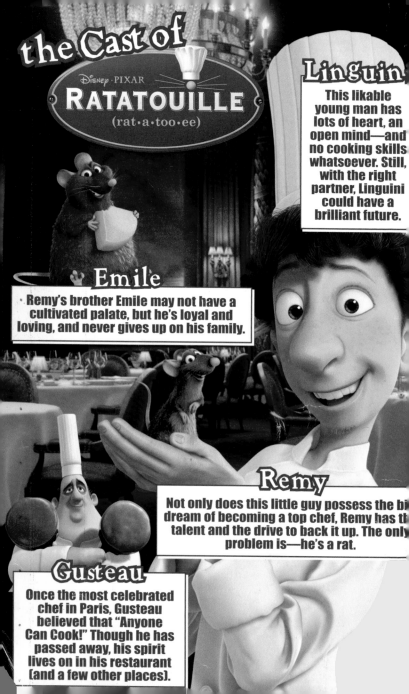

the Cast of

DISNEP · PIXAR
RATATOUILLE
(rat·a·too·ee)

Linguini

This likable young man has lots of heart, an open mind—and no cooking skills whatsoever. Still, with the right partner, Linguini could have a brilliant future.

Emile

Remy's brother Emile may not have a cultivated palate, but he's loyal and loving, and never gives up on his family.

Remy

Not only does this little guy possess the bi dream of becoming a top chef, Remy has th talent and the drive to back it up. The only problem is—he's a rat.

Gusteau

Once the most celebrated chef in Paris, Gusteau believed that "Anyone Can Cook!" Though he has passed away, his spirit lives on in his restaurant (and a few other places).

Colette

The only woman in Gusteau's kitchen, Colette has worked hard to get where she is. But beneath her tough exterior, Colette is kind and very smart. She's also an excellent cook.

Ego

The snobbiest food critic in Paris, Anton Ego wrote the review that took away one of Gusteau's five stars.

Skinner

Taking over after the kind Chef Gusteau, mean-spirited Skinner runs the kitchen with an iron fist and a quick temper.

Django

To Remy's dad, food isn't fabulous—it's just fuel. And though Django may not understand his son, he loves Remy and would do anything to keep him safe.

The best food in France is made in Paris...

And, some say, the best food in Paris is made by Chef Auguste Gusteau.

Gusteau's restaurant is the toast of Paris—booked five months in advance.

And his cookbook "Anyone Can Cook!" climbed to the top of the best-seller list.

But not everyone celebrates its success...

Amusing title, "Anyone Can Cook!" Gusteau actually seems to believe it.

I, on the other hand, take cooking seriously, and no—I don't think "anyone" can do it.

While the old lady who lived in the cottage slept nearby, Remy scrambled to find what he needed around her kitchen...

Saffron...saffron...

AUGUSTE GUSTEAU'S

She's gonna wake up.

Saffron will be just the thing. Gusteau swears by it.

Who's Gusteau?

Just the greatest chef in the world!

AUGUSTE GUSTEAU'S
Anyone CAN
COOK!

Wrote this cookbook.

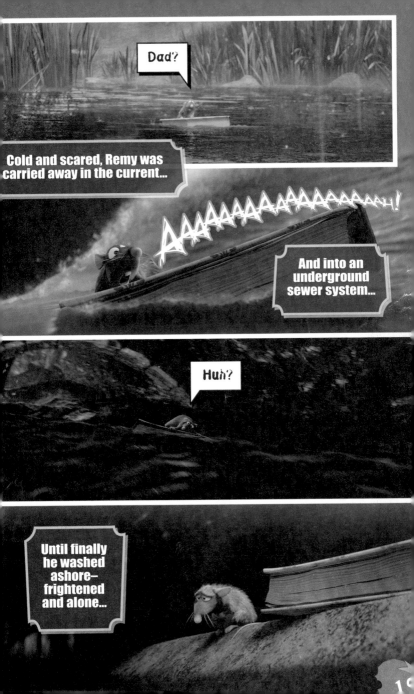

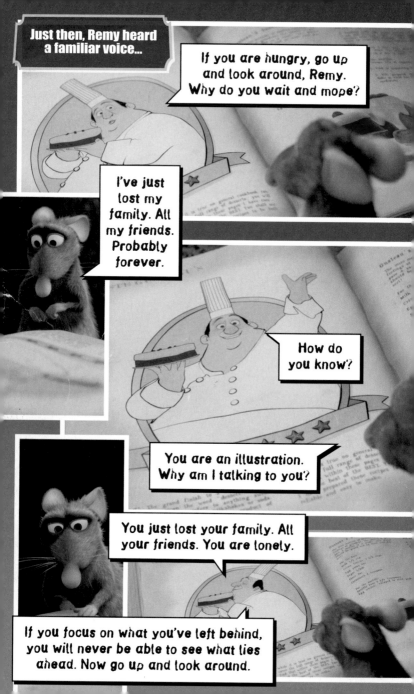

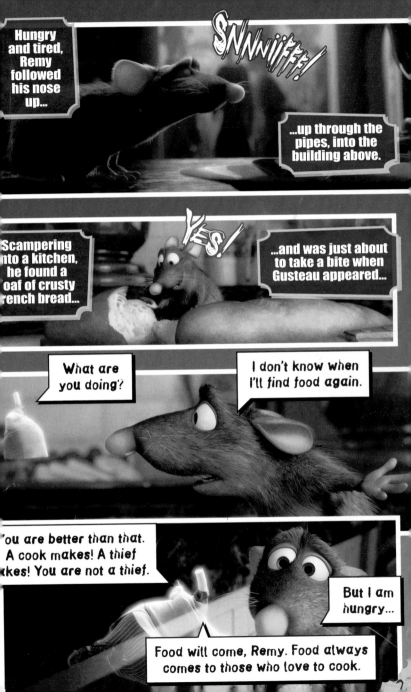

Climbing even higher up onto a rooftop, Remy took in the glittering

All this time I've been underneath Paris? Wow! It's beautiful!

And there was something else...

Gusteau's? You've led me to your restaurant?

It seems as though I have.

I gotta see this!

2

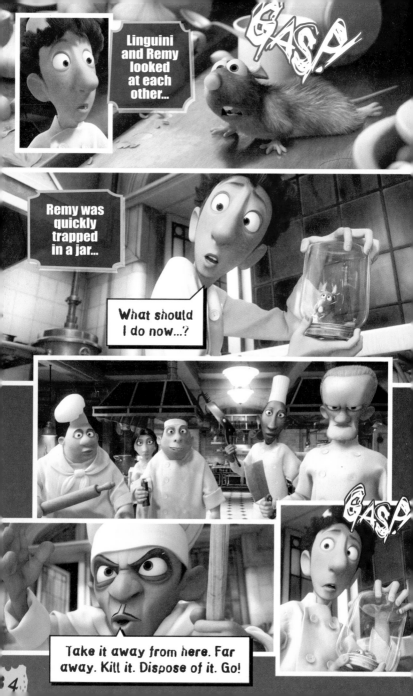

It wasn't long before they needed a better plan...

This is NOT going to work, Little Chef. We gotta figure out something else.

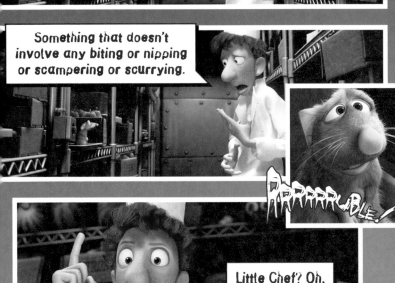

Something that doesn't involve any biting or nipping or scampering or scurrying.

GRRRRRUBLE!

Little Chef? Oh, you're hungry.

We just need to work out a system.

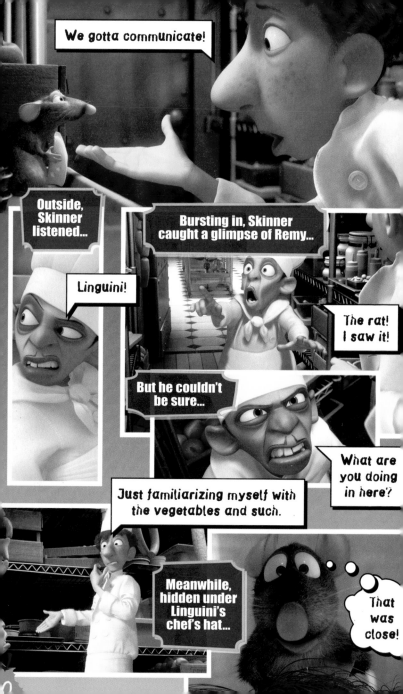

4

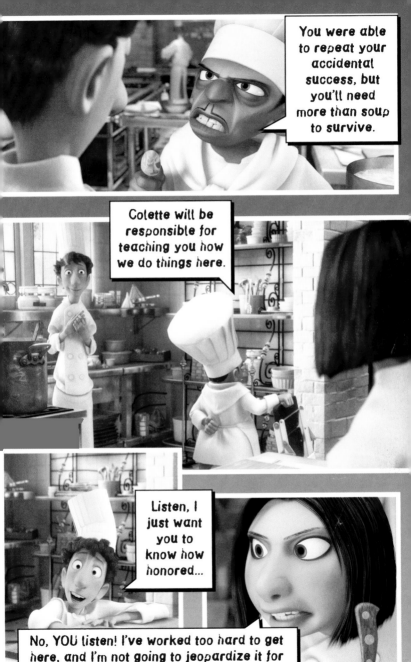

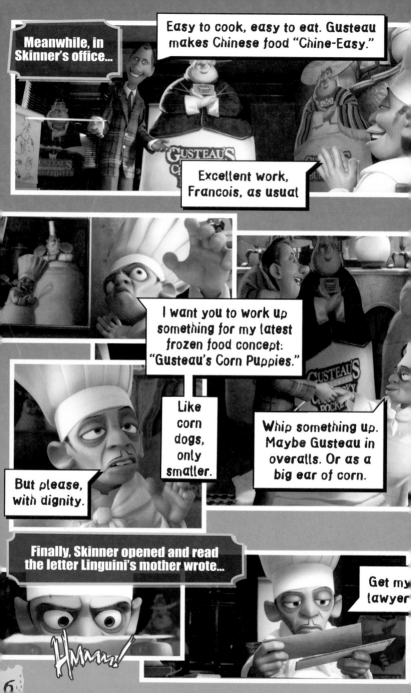

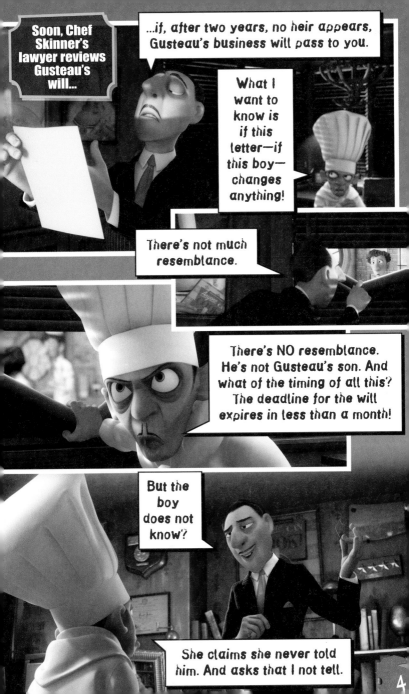

What does she want?

A job. For the boy.

Then what are you worried about?

The whole thing is highly suspect. He knows something!

Relax. He's a garbage boy. I think you can handle him.

After taking a stray hair from Gusteau's old chef's hat, the lawyer instructs Skinner to get a hair from Linguini, too! He's going to get a DNA test done.

8

People think haute cuisine is snooty, so chefs must also be snooty. But not so.

Lalo ran away from home. Horst has done time. Larousse ran guns for the resistance.

So you see, we are artists! Pirates! More than cooks are we.

We?

Oui, you are one of us now.

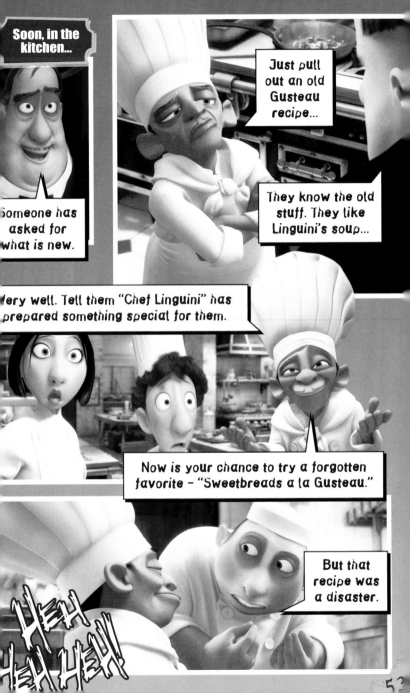

e are supposed to be preparing the Gusteau recipe. This is no time to experiment...

You're right. I should listen to you.

But hidden in Linguini's hat, Remy was insistent...

Don't you dare!

But before she could stop it, the dish was sent to the dining room...

Ignoring his father's warnings about how dangerous humans can be, Remy returned to the kitchen the next morning to find Linguini asleep on the floor. He'd stayed up all night cleaning the kitchen.

Just then, Colette's voice filled the kitchen...

BONJOUR!

Oh.

emy scurried nder Linguini's at, and tugged on Linguini's ir to make him nove. However, inguini would not wake up!

Good morning.

So. The Chef. He invited you in for a drink? That's big. What did he say?

What— you can't tell me?

Look, I'm no good with words.

I'm no good with food either. At least not without your help.

I hate false modesty. It's just another way to lie. You have talent—

GASP

No, but I don't. It's not me!

I have a secret. I have a raaaahhh,,,

You have a rash?

6

In the kitchen...

Distracted by his growing love for Colette, Linguini didn't pay much attention to Remy...

tuc!

No, try this. It's better.

As frustrating as the days were becoming, Remy also had troubles at night. His brother, Emile, kept bringing more and more hungry rats to Gusteau's.

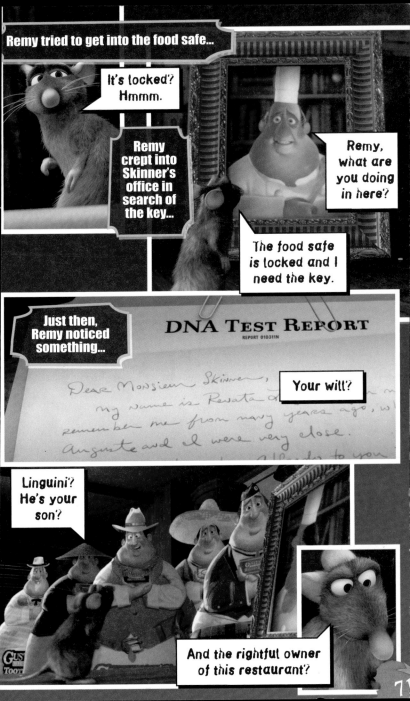

Outside, Skinner was waiting in the shadows.

He captured the tiny chef and gave him a terrible choice...

Remy could either help him create a line of Chef Skinner frozen food—or die!

GUSTEAU'S
MICROWAVE
CHOPSOCKY
POCKETS

Even worse, Remy soon found himself locked away in the trunk of Skinner's car.

There seemed to be no way he could get back to Gusteau's...

...to help Linguini on the biggest night of both of their lives!

GUSTEAU

That night at Gusteau's...

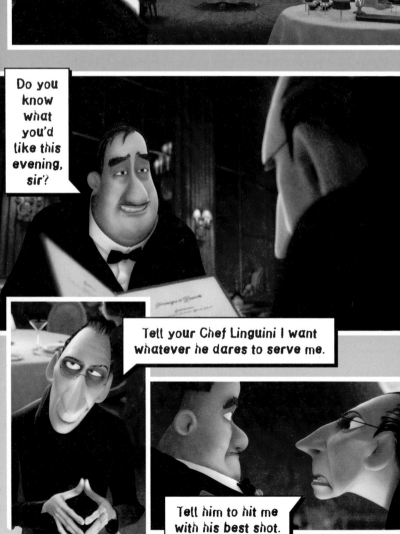

Do you know what you'd like this evening, sir?

Tell your Chef Linguini I want whatever he dares to serve me.

Tell him to hit me with his best shot.

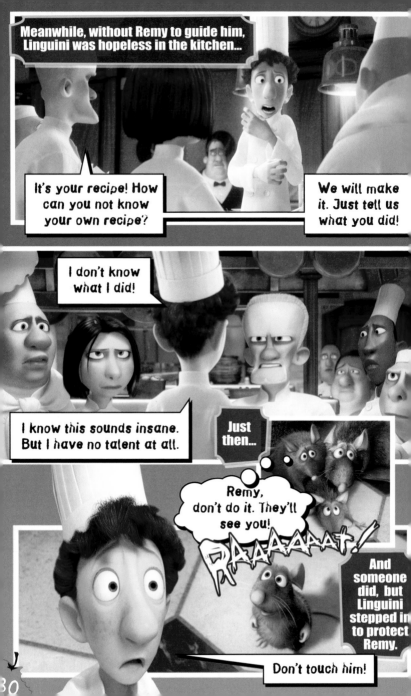

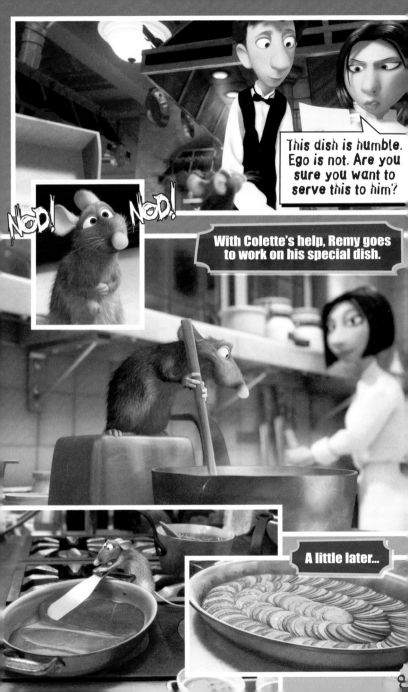

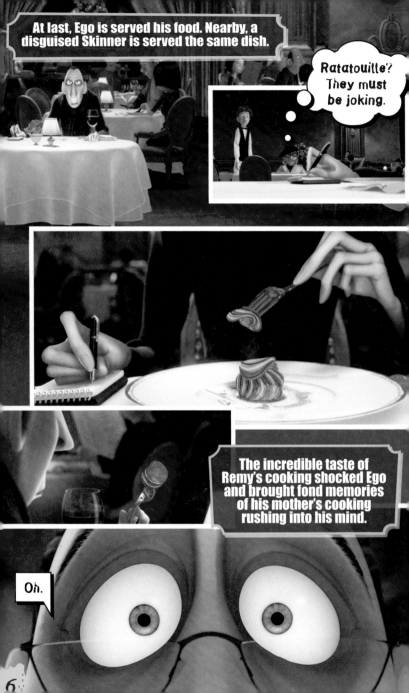

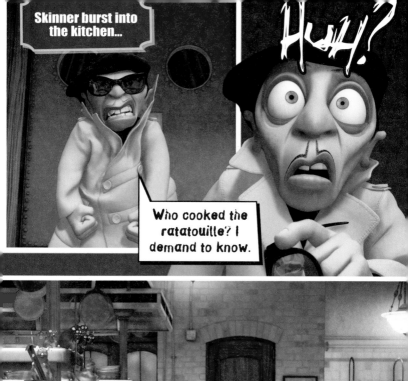

After the restaurant emptied, Colette and Linguini took Ego into the kitchen.

Thank you for the meal.

91

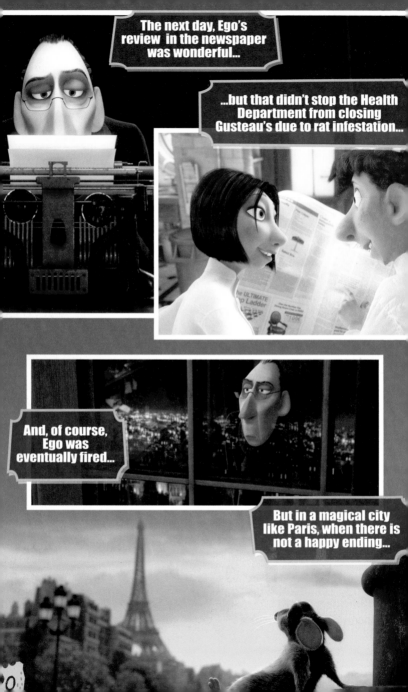

...you will find a happy beginning...

Remy, Linguini, olette and Ego opened a new restaurant...

Bring some food over here! We're starving!

...and reserved heir rooftop for rats only!

FIN!

Experience your favorite movies and TV shows in the palm of your hand...

...with TOKYOPOP® CINE-MANGA® books!

TOKYOPOP
DISNEY
HANNAH MONTANA
CINE-MANGA
DISNEY
HANNAH MONTANA
CINE-MANGA
TOKYOPOP
SECRETS AND SUPERSNEAKS
AVAILABLE NOW AT TOKYOPOP!
© Disney Enterprises, Inc.